Famous African-American Women

Illustrations by Cal Massey

Text by Janet Baine Kopito

DOVER PUBLICATIONS, INC.
Mineola, New York

Bibliographical Note

Famous African-American Women is a new work, first published by
Dover Publications, Inc., in 2002, and revised in 2010 and 2012.

International Standard Book Number

ISBN-13: 978-0-486-42052-3
ISBN-10: 0-486-42052-3

Manufactured in the United States by Courier Corporation
42052306   2014
www.doverpublications.com

INTRODUCTION

"What the people want is very simple. They want an America
as good as its promise."
—Barbara Jordan

"For I am my mother's daughter, and the drums of Africa still beat in my heart."
—Mary McLeod Bethune

The forty-five women who have been chosen for this book represent only a small part of the history of African-American women. Yet through their various life stories and numerous contributions and achievements, they give a true glimpse of what it means—and meant—to be an American woman of African heritage in the years spanning colonial America to the present day.

The women portrayed in this book developed their skills and talents in many areas: literature, law, public service, the performing arts, business, politics, and entertainment. Many of them achieved the distinction of being "first": Phillis Wheatley, first published African-American poet; Maggie Lena Walker, first African-American woman bank president; Hattie McDaniel, first African-American Academy Award winner. Several—Mary Ann Shadd Cary, Josephine St. Pierre Ruffin, Ida B. Wells Barnett, Maggie Lena Walker, and Daisy Bates—published newspapers in their eagerness to fight injustice and spread information of interest to African-Americans. A few, such as Josephine St. Pierre Ruffin and Mary Eliza Church Terrell, were involved in the development of African-American women's clubs—civic organizations formed to benefit the community. Two women— Coretta Scott King and Myrlie Evers-Williams—steadfastly carried on the cause of civil rights after the assassination of their husbands.

Some of the women were slaves or the daughters of slaves. Others came from privileged homes but were nonetheless committed to fighting for the rights and freedom of their sisters and brothers. Many are known for their courage—Harriet Tubman risking her own freedom to return again and again to slave states to lead men, women, and children to freedom; Ellen Craft, in a clever disguise, and her husband, William, fleeing from slavery; Bessie Coleman following her dream of becoming an aviator; Rosa Parks refusing to surrender her bus seat to a white passenger; and Ida B. Wells Barnett similarly refusing to give up her seat on a railroad train and suing the railroad after being ejected from the train. Many of the book's subjects were involved in both the anti-slavery and women's rights movements—the two causes were joined after the first National Women's Rights Convention in 1850.

Whether through the written word, the singing voice, the reach of the law, or many other modes of expression and influence, all of these women have greatly enriched the times they lived in, and the future to come.

"I speak to the black experience, but I am always talking about the human condition— about what we can endure, dream, fail at, and survive."
—Maya Angelou

Phillis Wheatley Born in West Africa, Phillis Wheatley [1753–1784] was kidnapped and sent to Boston as a child. John Wheatley and his wife, who purchased Phillis in 1761, raised her as one of their own children. Phillis learned to read and began making her way through the Bible and literary and historical works. She published her first poem in 1767 in a Rhode Island newspaper. In 1773, her only volume of poetry, *Poems on Various Subjects, Religious and Moral*, was published by an English company, making Phillis America's first published African-American poet. When doubts were raised that she was the poems' author, an "Attestation" was produced, with the signatures of the governor and lieutenant governor of Massachusetts, as well as John Hancock, affirming her authorship. Phillis Wheatley's achievements were taken by some to demonstrate that slaves, and Americans of African origin, were capable of "improving" themselves, had valuable contributions to make, and ought to live as free men and women.

Sojourner Truth Sojourner Truth [1797?–1883], the child of slaves, was born Isabel Baumfree in a Dutch settlement in upstate New York. She was sold several times, as well as being forced to marry an older slave, with whom she had five children. In 1843 she experienced a spiritual revelation and became a traveling preacher, using the expressive name Sojourner Truth. She worked with prominent Abolitionists and was active in the struggle to extend the vote to women. At the 1851 Women's Rights Convention in Akron, Ohio, Sojourner is said to have repeatedly uttered the words "And Ain't I a Woman?" to demonstrate her independence, hard work, and strength in the face of her life's trials. After the Civil War, Sojourner worked to help freed slaves establish new lives. She also took legal action to desegregate the streetcars of Washington, D.C. *The Narrative of Sojourner Truth*, written by Olive Gilbert "based on information provided by Sojourner Truth," was one of the first literary works to tell the life story of a female slave in America.

Harriet Tubman Born into slavery in Maryland, Harriet Tubman [1820?–1913] had a harsh childhood. She escaped to Philadelphia in 1849, leaving behind her husband. She then dedicated herself to rescuing other slaves, becoming a fearless "conductor" on the Underground Railroad—an assortment of routes and safe houses used to move slaves north to freedom. Often referred to as the "Moses of her people," Tubman returned to slave-holding states nearly twenty times in ten years to lead men, women, and children to freedom. She appeared at anti-slavery meetings and also was an outspoken supporter of women's rights. She served as a nurse and spy for the Union during the Civil War. Using money earned from speaking engagements and from the sale of her biography, *Harriet, Moses of her People*, written by Sarah Bradford, Harriet Tubman founded a home for impoverished elderly African Americans. She herself died in poverty.

Mary Ann Shadd Cary Mary Ann Shadd Cary [1823–1893] was born in Wilmington, Delaware, the first of thirteen children. Because it was illegal to educate African Americans in Delaware, Mary Ann's parents placed her in a Quaker boarding school in Pennsylvania. She returned to Delaware as a teenager and opened a private school for African Americans. After the 1850 passage of the Fugitive Slave Act—which permitted the capture of ex-slaves living in "free" states—Mary Ann and her brother fled to Canada; the rest of the family followed later. She wrote a pamphlet, "Notes on Canada," to let African Americans know about opportunities in Canada, and began publishing *The Provincial Freeman*, a weekly newspaper, in order to keep fugitive slaves informed. Her other achievements included opening an interracial school, serving as a recruiting officer to enlist African-American volunteers in the Union army during the Civil War, and earning a law degree in 1883. She was only the second African-American woman in the U.S. to earn a law degree.

Frances E. W. Harper Frances Ellen Watkins Harper [1825–1911] was born to free parents in Baltimore, Maryland. Orphaned at the age of three, she went to live with her uncle, a minister deeply committed to civil rights. Frances read widely in the library of the home where she worked as a nursemaid and began to write. Her poems appeared in 1839 in Abolitionist publications. In the 1850s she traveled through the U.S. and Canada speaking about slavery, racism, and women's rights. She got to know other activists, such as Sojourner Truth, Frederick Douglass, Harriet Tubman, and John Brown, through her activism. She donated part of the proceeds from her book *Poems on Miscellaneous Subjects* to the Underground Railroad movement. In 1859 she published "The Two Officers," becoming the first African-American to publish a short story. In 1866 she spoke at the National Women's Rights Convention. Frances Harper's most popular work is *Iola Leroy: On Shadows Uplifted*, one of the first novels published by an African-American woman in the United States.

Ellen Craft Born in Clinton, Georgia, in 1826, this daughter of a slave and her owner was presented to her half-sister as a wedding gift when she was eleven years old. She married William Craft, a slave, in 1846. Ellen and William made a daring escape from slavery in 1848: she disguised herself as a white gentleman, accompanied by his slave—her husband, William! Their destination was Boston, the center of the Abolitionist movement. However, the Fugitive Slave Act (1850) permitted the capture of ex-slaves living in free states, and the Crafts decided to move to England, where they lived for 17 years. They returned home after the Civil War to open a cooperative farm—it was destroyed by the Ku Klux Klan—and a school, where Ellen taught. William Craft's first-person account of their escape, *Running a Thousand Miles for Freedom*, was published in 1860. Ellen Craft died in 1891.

Mary Elizabeth Bowser Mary Elizabeth Bowser was born into slavery around 1839 on a Virginia plantation. The owner's daughter, a Quaker and Abolitionist, sent Mary Elizabeth to Philadelphia to be educated. While working as a servant at the home of Jefferson Davis in the Confederate White House, she was able to help the Union effort by gathering and transmitting details about Confederate war plans to Union spies. Mary Elizabeth was said to have had a "photographic" mind that enabled her to absorb useful information. She also reported on the contents of many conversations that she overheard while going about her daily chores. Unfortunately, little is known about her life after the war, and her date of death is unknown. Her contribution to the Union war effort, however, was considerable.

Josephine St. Pierre Ruffin Born in Boston, Josephine St. Pierre [1842–1924] attended an out-of-town integrated school rather than her local segregated school. In 1858 she married George Lewis Ruffin, the first African-American graduate of Harvard Law School. Josephine supported women's right to vote, joining forces with Susan B. Anthony and Julia Ward Howe. After writing for a weekly African-American newspaper, she published *Woman's Era*, the country's first paper for African-American women. She also organized the Woman's Era Club; its motto was "Make the World Better." Josephine went on to organize the National Federation of Afro-American Women, a gathering of African-American women's clubs. She was barred from representing an all-African-American club at the General Federation of Women's Clubs meeting in Milwaukee in 1900. Told that she could represent white clubs, she refused, an act known as the "Ruffin Incident."

Mary Eliza Mahoney Mary Eliza Mahoney [1845–1926] was born in Boston to a family that had relocated to the free state of Massachusetts from the slave-holding state of North Carolina. She worked at the New England Hospital for Women and Children in various jobs, including unofficial nurse's assistant. She graduated from the hospital's Training School for Nurses in 1879, becoming America's first African-American graduate nurse. At that time, nurses were expected to perform household tasks such as washing and ironing clothes and cleaning, in addition to their nursing duties. Mary Eliza Mahoney rejected this practice and fought for nurses to be respected as professionals. She was inducted into the Nursing Hall of Fame in 1976, and into the National Women's Hall of Fame in 1993. The Mary Mahoney Award is given to a person or group who has promoted integration within the nursing profession.

Susie Baker King Taylor Susie Baker King Taylor [1848–1912] was born a slave near Savannah, Georgia. After Susie was freed, she was assigned to do the laundry for the 33rd U.S. Colored Troops during the Civil War. At the age of 14, she married Edward King, a sergeant in the regiment. Having pieced together an education from obliging friends and neighbors, she was able to teach her husband's regiment to read and write. In her autobiography, *A Black Woman's* *Civil War Memoirs: Reminiscences of my life in camp with the 33rd United States Colored Troops late 1st S.C. Volunteers,* she states that she was never paid for tutoring the soldiers, but was always glad to do so because she was permitted to care for "the sick and afflicted comrades." She continued her interest in nursing after the war, helping to found a branch of the Woman's Relief Corps.

Anna Julia Haywood Cooper The daughter of an African slave, Anna Julia Haywood Cooper was born in Raleigh, North Carolina, in 1858. She showed a thirst for knowledge at an early age and began tutoring students in Raleigh when still a child. She attended Oberlin College in Ohio with Mary Eliza Church Terrell (page 16), where she was one of the first African-American women to complete a four-year course at an accredited American college. She believed in improving educational opportunities for African-American girls and women, and was dedicated to shaping an American education system that would address the needs of African-American students. In 1925 she earned a Ph.D. from the Sorbonne University in Paris, becoming one of the first African-American woman to do so. A collection of her writings, *A Voice from the South by a Black Woman of the South*, was published in 1892. She died in 1964.

Ida B. Wells Barnett Ida B. Wells Barnett [1862–1931] was born a slave in Holly Springs, Mississippi. After her parents died when she was 14, Ida took teaching jobs to help the family. Her activism began in 1884 when she decided not to give up her seat on a railroad train to a white passenger. After she was removed from the train, she hired an attorney and sued the railroad. She won initially, but the Tennessee Supreme Court reversed the ruling. She found her voice as a journalist, and, as the editor of the African-American publication *The Free Speech and Headlight*, she spoke out against racial injustice. Her book *The Red Record* was the first work to compile statistics about lynching. Ida participated in the 1913 march to Washington, D.C., for women's suffrage and was a founding member of the NAACP. She was one of the first African-American women to run for public office in her bid to join the Illinois state legislature.

Mary Eliza Church Terrell Mary Eliza Church Terrell [1863–1954], above left, was born in Memphis, Tennessee, to former slaves. Her father's successful real estate ventures made him the first African-American millionaire in Memphis. Mary Eliza earned bachelor's and master's degrees from Oberlin College, Ohio, where she was acquainted with Anna Julia Haywood Cooper (page 14). The Terrells named their daughter after the eighteenth-century poet Phillis Wheatley (page 4). The lynching of a childhood friend led to Mary Eliza's commitment to social activism. She was involved in the African-American women's club movement, supported the issues of women's voting rights and minority employment, and was a founding member of the NAACP. While in her late eighties, Mary Eliza joined in protests to integrate restaurants in Washington, D.C.; the Supreme Court ruled against discrimination in public restaurants in 1953.

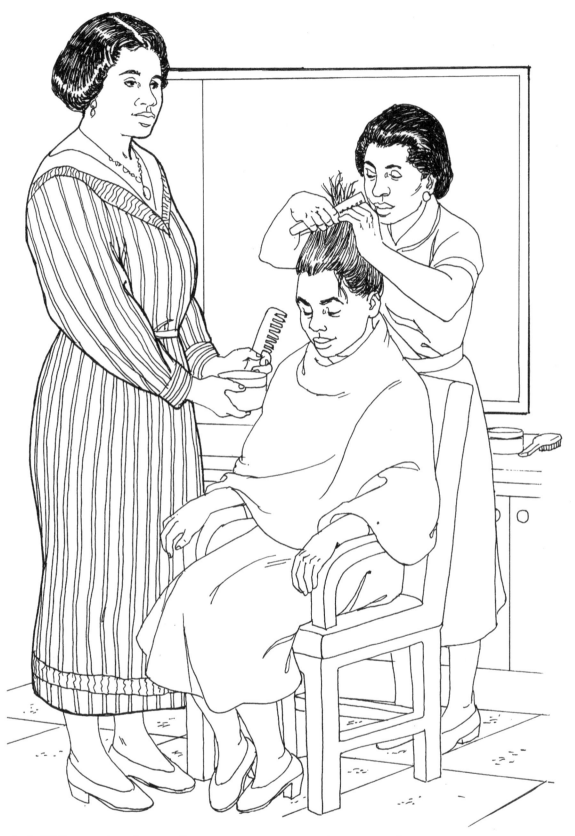

Madam C. J. Walker Madam C. J. Walker [1867–1919], above left, was born Sarah Breedlove in Delta, Louisiana, to former slaves. She worked in the cotton fields after her parents died, married at fourteen, and was widowed several years later. Sarah moved with her young daughter to St. Louis, where her brothers worked as barbers. To help arrest her own hair loss, she developed Madam Walker's Wonderful Hair Grower and began doing business as Madam C. J. Walker. She handled both the sales and marketing of her products and traveled the country performing demonstrations. Through her tireless efforts and ambition, she became the first African-American woman to be a millionaire. Madam Walker was active in the anti-lynching movement, speaking at NAACP fund-raisers, and urged fellow businesswomen to fight for justice through political involvement.

Maggie Lena Walker Maggie Lena Walker was born in 1867 in Richmond, Virginia, to former slaves. The house they lived in had been a "station" on the Underground Railroad. Maggie, an outstanding student, taught briefly after graduating high school. Real opportunity arrived, however, when she took a job with the Independent Order of St. Luke, a religious service organization for African Americans. Maggie proved to be an excellent manager, and she transformed the impoverished organization into a thriving enterprise. She founded the St. Luke Penny Savings Bank (today the Consolidated Bank and Trust Company) and was the first woman to be a bank president in the U.S. She established the *St. Luke Herald* newspaper, a voice for African Americans and a tool for social commentary that she edited for thirty years. Maggie Lena Walker lent a hand to numerous civic organizations benefiting African-Americans in Richmond and was national director of the NAACP. She died in 1934.

From the first,
I made my learning,
little as it was,
useful every way
I could —

Mary McLeod Bethune

Mary McLeod Bethune The daughter of slaves, Mary McLeod Bethune [1875–1955] was born on a farm near Mayesville, South Carolina. An excellent student, she was sent to school in North Carolina by a benefactor and received a scholarship to Moody Bible Institute in North Carolina. After marrying, she moved to Florida to manage a new mission school, but dreamed of opening her own school for African American girls. In 1904 she did just that, furnishing the school with discarded items. Eventually, Mary's Daytona Educational and Industrial Training School became a 32-acre, coeducational campus—Bethune-Cookman College. In 1912 Mary joined the Equal Suffrage League and worked for women's right to vote. She served as president of organizations such as the National Council of Negro Women and became the first African-American woman to direct a federal agency (1936). In 1974, nearly one hundred years after her birth, a statue was erected in her honor in Washington, D.C. She was the first woman, and first African American, to receive this honor.

Zora Neale Hurston Zora Neale Hurston was born in Notasulga, Alabama, in 1891, but she grew up in Eatonville, Florida. Zora joined a traveling theater at sixteen and also did domestic work for a white family. Her employer gave Zora her first book and enrolled her in high school in Baltimore. Zora attended Howard University, leaving with a two-year degree. She began entering writing contests and publishing her stories. Moving to New York in 1925, she became part of the Harlem Renaissance—the African-American arts movement that included poet Langston Hughes and novel- ist Nella Larsen. Zora studied anthropology at Columbia University. Using that training, she returned to Eatonville and also traveled through remote areas of the South collecting African-American and African folklore, which she used in her writing; she became an authority on folk music as well. Zora Neale Hurston published four novels, including *Their Eyes Were Watching God*, and an autobiography, *Dust Tracks on a Road*, in the 1930s and early 1940s. Her later years were marked by personal troubles, and she died in poverty in Fort Pierce, Florida, in 1960.

Bessie Coleman Bessie Coleman, the first African-American woman to fly a plane, was born in 1892 in Atlanta, Texas. To escape her family's poverty she moved to Chicago, where she worked as a manicurist. Bessie was intrigued by accounts of World War I air battles, as well as by tales of French women aviators. When Bessie was rejected by American aviation schools, she went abroad and got her pilot's license in France (1921). She completed an advanced course the following year, becoming the first woman to receive an International Aviation license—as well as the world's first African-

American aviator. Bessie joined air shows after returning to the U.S., insisting that African-American spectators be let in through the same gates as whites. She traveled the country encouraging young African Americans to pursue their dreams in aviation. Finally able to afford her own plane in 1926, Bessie went for a test flight with her mechanic. The plane malfunctioned, and Bessie fell from the cockpit; she and her mechanic were killed. In 1995, the U.S. Postal Service issued a stamp commemorating Bessie Coleman's fearless pursuit of her dream.

Hattie McDaniel Hattie McDaniel [1895–1952] was born in Wichita, Kansas. She displayed singing talent as a child and began traveling with minstrel and vaudeville troupes. While performing at a Milwaukee nightclub where she was an employee, Hattie dazzled the patrons with her singing voice. The club provided her with a showcase for her talents for a year. Opportunities opened up for her, and she became the first African-American woman to sing on network radio.

In 1931 she moved to Los Angeles, seeking to advance her career. She appeared in her first movie in 1932. But she achieved stardom with her performance in the Civil War epic *Gone With the Wind* (1939). Hattie won an Academy Award for Best Supporting Actress, making her the first African American to win the Oscar. Dozens of Hollywood films followed, including *Showboat* and *Song of the South*. She also had a successful career in radio and television.

Ethel Waters Ethel Waters was born in Chester, Pennsylvania, in 1896 (some sources say 1900). She made her singing "debut" at the age of five, performing in a church program. Traveling with carnivals and vaudeville shows, Ethel impressed spectators with her rich singing voice. She was known as "Sweet Mama Stringbean" early in her career because of her tall, narrow frame. Ethel Waters was one of America's first jazz singers. She began her recording career in 1921 and successfully toured numerous cities as a jazz performer. She was included in the star billing with white actors for the Broadway show *As Thousands Cheered*; Irving Berlin wrote several musical numbers for her. Ethel Waters performed at Carnegie Hall in 1938. Her films include *Pinky* (1949) and *A Member of the Wedding* (1952). She was nominated for Best Supporting Actress Academy Awards for both roles. She died in 1977.

Marian Anderson Born in Philadelphia, Pennsylvania, Marian Anderson [1897–1993] so impressed people with her vocal talent that her church raised money to pay for her voice lessons. She experienced racial prejudice when applying to a music school; instead, she took private lessons, for which she was not charged. After performing at Town Hall in New York, Marian traveled to Europe, where she performed for ten years. She then returned to the U.S. in 1935 for another recital at Town Hall. As an African-American performer, Marian met with discrimination at restaurants, hotels, and concert halls. When she was denied an engagement in Washington, D.C., First Lady Eleanor Roosevelt helped arrange a concert for Marian on the steps of the Lincoln Memorial. She performed to an audience of 75,000 in this stand against racism. In 1955, she became the first African-American member of the Metropolitan Opera to sing an important role. Marian Anderson received the Presidential Medal of Freedom in 1963.

Clara "Mother" Hale Clara Hale was born in Elizabeth City, North Carolina, in 1905. A teenage orphan and a widow at twenty-seven, Clara began taking in children for day care in the 1930s. This arrangement enabled her to earn a living while remaining at home with her three children. She proved to be a nurturing presence in the children's lives, and over time was a foster parent to forty children. She gave up being a foster parent when she was in her sixties. However, at that point in her life she found her greatest challenge because of an incident in her daughter, Lorraine's, life. Lorraine sent a drug-addicted mother who could not care for her child to Clara Hale, who took in the child. Soon, other mothers were availing themselves of Mother Hale's concern and generosity by leaving their children at Clara Hale's apartment. Clara insisted that the mothers enter rehabilitation or demonstrate that they were capable of caring for their children before they could reclaim them. Eventually she received government funding and was able to open Hale House in Harlem, New York. Mother Hale died in 1992.

Katherine Dunham Born in Joliet, Illinois, in 1909, Katherine Dunham became interested in music and dance after a cousin took her to a local theater. Her fascination with anthropology led her to study at the University of Chicago, where she earned bachelor's, master's, and doctoral degrees in that subject. She was one of the university's first African-American students. In 1931 she opened her first dance studio. A fellowship enabled her to travel to Haiti and Jamaica, where she used her training in anthropology to investigate African-influenced Caribbean dance forms. A social activist, Katherine Dunham developed a program in East St. Louis that enabled community members to experience the arts firsthand and explore many different cultures, including that of Africa. She received the Presidential Medal of Arts and the NAACP Lifetime Achievement Award. She died in 2006.

Mahalia Jackson Known as America's greatest gospel singer, Mahalia Jackson was born in 1911 in New Orleans, Louisiana. The grandchild of slaves, she was raised by an extended family that included musicians and entertainers. In addition, she benefited from the flourishing music scene in New Orleans. Mahalia loved to sing spirituals and the blues but would not record religious songs, although she did perform them at churches and conventions. In 1947, she became the official soloist with the National Baptist Convention. By 1954 she had her own radio and TV programs. Two of Mahalia Jackson's best-known recordings are "He's Got the Whole World in His Hands" and "When the Saints Go Marching In." A strong supporter of Dr. Martin Luther King, Jr., and the civil rights movement, she performed at the 1963 March on Washington, as well as at Dr. King's funeral. Her performances took her to Europe, Africa, India, and Asia. She died in 1972.

Rosa Parks Rosa Parks was born in 1913 in Tuskegee, Alabama. With a simple act of disobedience in 1955, Rosa changed the course of the American civil rights movement. The law in Montgomery, Alabama, decreed that African-American bus riders give up their seats to whites. Rosa Parks was prepared to face the consequences when a bus driver demanded that she give up her seat to a white passenger; she was promptly arrested. A boycott was organized, with the participation of Martin Luther King, Jr., and Montgomery's bus system, heavily dependent on African-American riders, suffered great financial losses. With Rosa's approval, her lawyer took the case to the U.S. Supreme Court. Almost a year later, in November 1956, the court ruled that the segregation laws were unconstitutional. Called the "Mother of the Civil Rights Movement," Mrs. Parks founded the Rosa and Raymond Parks Institute for Self Development, a nonprofit organization that helps young people develop positive goals. She died in 2005.

Daisy Bates Daisy Bates was born in Huttig, Arkansas, in 1914(?). She first encountered racial discrimination when told by a grocer that she would have to wait until the white customers were taken care of. She was only seven, but she had experienced discrimination firsthand. As an adult, she and her husband, a journalist and insurance salesman, founded the civil rights-oriented *Arkansas Free Press* (1941). The paper contained articles about police brutality and the poor treatment of African-American World War II veterans. By speaking out, Daisy Bates and her husband helped improve living conditions for African Americans in Arkansas. In 1957, Daisy Bates took up the cause of nine African-American students who were scheduled to attend Central High School in Little Rock, amid threats of violence. Although the Supreme Court had ruled school segregation unconstitutional in 1954, Arkansas Governor Faubus vowed to resist attempts to desegregate the schools. The *Arkansas Free Press* was boycotted and had to shut down in 1959. Daisy continued her activism, moving to Washington, D.C., to participate in President Johnson's anti-poverty programs. She died in 1999.

Gwendolyn Brooks Gwendolyn Brooks was born in 1917 in Topeka, Kansas, but grew up in Chicago. An enthusiastic reader, she tried her hand at creative writing, and, by the age of sixteen, had published over seventy poems. After studying English at junior college, she became publicity director of a local NAACP Youth Council. She began attending poetry workshops and published her first collection of poems, *A Street in Bronzeville*, in 1945. The subject of the poems was the lives of the people of the Bronzeville neighborhood of Chicago. Her 1949 book *Annie Allen* earned her a Pulitzer Prize, the first awarded to an African-American writer. Gwendolyn Brooks brought poetry to the people, lecturing and reading verse at schools and in prisons. The recipient of many awards and honorary degrees, she died in 2000.

Ella Fitzgerald Born in Newport News, Virginia, in 1917, young Ella lost her parents as a teenager and was sent to an orphanage in New York. In 1934, she performed at Amateur Night at the Apollo Theater in Harlem, winning prize money, as well as a job with a band, for her outstanding vocal ability. She was hired by Chick Webb to sing with his orchestra, and her performing career took off. After Webb died, Ella took over the band. She made a name for herself with improvisation and "scat"—a style of singing in which the human voice imitates a musical instrument, using sounds instead of words. Ella's wide vocal range enabled her to master this difficult method. Throughout her career, she recorded the songs of George Gershwin, Irving Berlin, Duke Ellington, and other greats, and she performed at jazz festivals and concert halls. Her health was failing by the 1990s; she died in 1996.

Constance Baker Motley Born in 1921 to West Indian immigrant parents in New Haven, Connecticut, Constance Baker Motley decided upon a law career after high school. Her college education was funded by a man who heard her give a speech while she was an employee of the National Youth Administration. She graduated from New York University with a degree in economics, later attending Columbia Law School and becoming a law clerk for Thurgood Marshall in the NAACP Legal Defense and Educational Fund in New York. One of her successful civil rights cases involved James Meredith's attempt to attend the University of Mississippi in 1962. Her legal triumphs led to her involvement in politics. Constance Baker Motley was the first female African-American senator (New York State, 1964–65); the first woman to be borough president; and the first African-American woman appointed to a federal judgeship. She was inducted into the National Women's Hall of Fame in 1993 and died in 2005.

Shirley Chisholm Shirley Chisholm was born to a West Indian immigrant family in Brooklyn in 1924. She earned a master's degree in elementary education after attending graduate school on scholarships. In her early years, she was a teacher and a day-care administrator. She set her sights on improving inner-city conditions and securing civil rights and women's rights. Shirley and her first husband were active in local politics, forming the Unity Democratic Club in 1960 in an attempt to get African-American and Hispanic voters to the polls. She won a state assembly seat in New York in 1964 and was the first African-American woman to sit in the House of Representatives (1969). In the 1960s, she supported the creation of the SEEK program, which greatly increased minority enrollment at the City and State University of New York four-year colleges. Her book *Unbought and Unbossed* was published in 1970; *The Good Fight* appeared in 1973. She died in 2005 at the age of eighty.

Althea Gibson Althea Gibson was born in 1927 in Silver, South Carolina, but she grew up in Harlem, where her family moved when she was a small child. She began taking tennis lessons at Harlem's Cosmopolitan Club when she was fourteen and won her first tournament in 1942, playing in the American Tennis Association, an African-American organization. As an African-American player, she was barred from public tennis courts, but a doctor who was aware of her talent arranged for her to play on his private court. In 1950 she became the first African American to compete at the U.S. National Tournament (now the U.S. Open), at the request of a former tournament winner, Alice Marble. In 1951 Althea broke the race barrier when she competed at Wimbledon in England. She continued to win championships throughout the 1950s, including the U.S. Nationals in 1957 and 1958. Her autobiography, *I Always Wanted to Be Somebody*, was published in 1958. Althea Gibson died in 2003.

Coretta Scott King Coretta Scott King was born in 1927 on the family farm in Heiberger, Alabama, where she spent her childhood. She enrolled at Antioch College in Ohio, where her sister had been the first full-time African-American student to live on campus. After Coretta was barred from student teaching at local public schools, she pursued a career as a professional singer and was accepted to the New England Conservatory of Music in Boston. There she met Martin Luther King, Jr., who was also a student in Boston. They married in 1953. The Kings moved to Alabama, where Martin became a minister. His fight for civil rights meant danger for the family, including the firebombing of their house in 1965. By then they had four children. Coretta continued her political involvement after her husband's assassination in 1968. In 1969, as a monument to her husband, she brought about the construction in Atlanta of the Martin Luther King, Jr., Center for Nonviolent Social Change. She published *My Life With Martin Luther King Jr.* in 1969. Coretta Scott King died in 2006.

Leontyne Price Born in 1927 in Laurel, Mississippi, Leontyne Price showed musical talent at an early age. She began taking piano lessons when she was five. She attended college in Ohio, planning to be a music teacher, but ultimately enrolled at the Juilliard School of Music in New York on a full scholarship. She made her Broadway debut in 1952. In 1955 Leontyne Price became the first African-American singer to appear in an opera on television. Some local stations canceled the program in protest. By 1957 she had appeared in her first stage opera, and she made her debut at the Metropolitan Opera House in New York in 1961. Her many recordings and international renown made her the first African-American singer to gain "superstar" status. In 1985 she retired from the Met but continued to give recitals. In 1964 Leontyne Price was awarded the Presidential Medal of Freedom, the highest award given to a civilian, by President Lyndon Johnson.

Maya Angelou Although she is known primarily as a writer, Maya Angelou has been a dancer, a singer, an editor, and an actor. She was born in St. Louis, Missouri, in 1928. Pursuing a dream, Maya became the first African-American streetcar conductor in San Francisco. In the 1950s she studied dance in New York; she then worked as a teacher, writer, and editor in Egypt and Ghana. Maya published *I Know Why the Caged Bird Sings*, the first part of her autobiography, in 1970 (four more volumes followed). She became involved with African-American political movements in the 1960s and was asked by Dr. Martin Luther King, Jr., to be the Northern coordinator of the Southern Christian Leadership Conference. She published poetry in the 1970s and became a professor of American Studies, with a lifetime appointment, at Wake Forest University in 1981. In 1993 she was asked by Bill Clinton to give a reading at his presidential inauguration. Maya recited the poem "On the Pulse of Morning," which she had written for the occasion.

Lorraine Hansberry Lorraine Hansberry was born in Chicago in 1930. Her parents won a civil rights case after encountering racism when buying a house in a white neighborhood. As a student, Lorraine studied art, but she found herself drawn to writing, and she moved to New York in 1950 to establish a literary career. While holding a job at the African-American newspaper *Freedom*, Lorraine worked on her own writing projects. Her best-known work, the play *A Raisin in the Sun*, was first produced on Broadway in 1959. Lorraine Hansberry became the first African-American author to win the New York Drama Critics Circle Award for best play of the year. A movie version of the drama was made in 1961, and a musical, *Raisin*, in 1973. Lorraine chose lines from Langston Hughes' poem "Dream Deferred" for her play's title: "What happens to a dream deferred?/Does it dry up/like a raisin in the sun?" Lorraine Hansberry died in 1965. Her husband gathered her writings together into a dramatic production, *To Be Young, Gifted, and Black*, which was first produced in 1969.

Toni Morrison Toni Morrison was born in Lorain, Ohio, in 1931. As a child she was an avid reader whose enjoyment of literature was enriched by her family's tradition of storytelling. Toni attended Howard University with an interest in education. She studied English and classical literature and obtained a master's degree from Cornell University. She taught in Texas and then returned to Howard to teach English. She then took a job as an editor in New York; meanwhile, her own writing flourished. She found a publisher for her novel *The Bluest Eye* in 1970 after many rejections. This early effort was followed by *Sula*, *Song of Solomon*, and *Jazz*. In addition to her own novels, Toni Morrison has helped support the writing efforts of other African Americans. She received the Pulitzer Prize for her novel *Beloved* in 1988. Oprah Winfrey both produced and starred in the 1998 movie version of the novel. In 1993, Toni Morrison became the first African American to receive the Nobel Prize in Literature.

Myrlie Evers-Williams Myrlie Evers-Williams was born in Vicksburg, Mississippi, in 1933. She met Medgar Evers while attending college, and they married in 1951. Myrlie and Medgar worked for the Mississippi NAACP, organizing voter registration drives. Registering to vote was a dangerous—and courageous—act for African Americans, as their names and addresses might be listed in the newspaper, leading to harassment. As the couple became more active in the civil rights movement, they became the targets of violence. They used codes and disguises to move about, expecting the worst but refusing to quit their efforts. On June 12, 1963, a day after President Kennedy's plea for racial harmony, Medgar Evers was shot in front of his house. His accused murderer was tried and acquitted. Myrlie moved the family to California, where she became the first woman on the Board of Public Works. She continued her efforts to have the murder case reopened, and, in 1994—over 30 years later—her husband's killer was convicted. In 1995, Myrlie Evers became the first woman to chair the NAACP. She published her memoir, *Watch Me Fly*, in 1999.

Barbara Jordon A politician whose career was marked by many firsts, Barbara Jordan was born in 1936 in Houston, Texas. She attended Phillis Wheatley High School in Houston, excelling on the debate team and graduating with honors. A presentation at a career day led to her interest in a career in law. She received a law degree from Boston University in 1959. Barbara taught at the University of Texas at Austin for many years. She was the first African-American woman to be elected to the Texas Senate. She used her governmental position to sponsor bills benefiting the disadvantaged. She also brought about improvements in workers' compensation benefits. In 1994 she was awarded the Presidential Medal of Freedom by President Clinton. Barbara Jordan died in 1996.

Marian Wright Edelman Marian Wright Edelman was born in Bennettsville, South Carolina, in 1939. She grew up in a family that made nightly study sessions a part of their daily routine. Her father required that his children take part in community service as well. Marian attended Spelman College, the first college for African-American women. The civil rights movement was underway, and Marian helped organize protests. She also became involved in Head Start, the pre-kindergarten program developed in 1965 to prepare low-income children for school. She was drawn to the law and graduated from Yale University Law School in 1963. Marian Wright Edelman was the first African-American woman to pass the bar examination in Mississippi. A tireless voice for America's children, she founded the non-profit Children's Defense Fund in 1973. Her book *A Measure of Our Success: A Letter to My Children & Yours*, published in 1992, was a *New York Times* bestseller. She received the Presidential Medal of Freedom in 2000.

Wilma Rudolph Wilma Rudolph was born in 1940 in Clarksville, Tennessee. After many childhood illnesses and a bout with polio, Wilma underwent physical therapy. It was uncertain whether she would ever walk again. However, after working hard to regain her physical strength, she decided to become an athlete. She excelled in track at high school—she was an undefeated sprinter—as well as basketball. In 1960, Wilma was the first American woman to win three Olympic gold medals in track events. She demanded that her homecoming in Tennessee be integrated, and, later on, joined protests against segregation laws. She was the first female athlete to attend the invitational Millrose Games, as well as the New York Athletic Club Track Meet. In 1967, at the invitation of Vice President Humphrey, Wilma took part in Operation Champ, an outreach program that involved underprivileged children in sports. She wrote an autobiography, *Wilma*, in 1977. Wilma Rudolph died in 1994.

Nikki Giovanni Nikki Giovanni was born in 1943 in Knoxville, Tennessee, but was raised in Oklahoma. She attended Fisk University, where her studies were interrupted because of her outspoken nature; she went on to graduate in 1967. She was active in the Student Nonviolent Coordinating Committee (SNCC) and became part of the Black Arts Movement and Black Power Movement. In 1968 she published her first volume of poetry, *Black Feeling, Black Talk*. She has continued to write poems, some for children, exploring what is means to be an African American. In 1971 Nikki published a collection of autobiographical essays entitled *Gemini: An Extended Biographical Statement on My First Twenty-Five Years at Being a Black Poet*. During the 1970s she traveled widely, giving many poetry readings. She has also made many recordings of her poetry. In 1989 she accepted a teaching position at the Virginia Polytechnic Institute as an English instructor. She has received the NAACP Image Award and the Langston Hughes Award for Distinguished Contributions to Arts and Letters.

Oprah Winfrey Born in Kosciusko, Mississippi, in 1954, Oprah Winfrey had a difficult childhood, being moved from one family member's home to another as a child. However, she graduated from college on a scholarship and went on to work in radio and television as reporter, news anchor (she was the first African-American anchor at WTVF in Nashville), and co-host. Her big career breakthrough came when she took over a morning TV show in Chicago in 1984. Its success led to the hour-long "Oprah Winfrey Show." This often controversial program nevertheless gave the audience and viewers an opportunity to discuss issues troubling society. Oprah's efforts led to President Clinton's signing of the "Oprah" bill—legislation designed to protect children from abuse. Oprah has also pursued an acting career, receiving an Academy Award nomination for her role in the film *The Color Purple* (1985). In 1998 she both produced and starred in the film version of Toni Morrison's Pulitzer Prize-winning novel *Beloved*. She started a book club in 1996, resulting in widespread readership of her "picks." *Time* magazine named Oprah Winfrey one of the 100 Most Influential People of the Twentieth Century in 1998.

Mae Jemison Mae Jemison—the first African-American woman to travel into space—was born in 1956 in Decatur, Alabama. She became interested in the sciences at an early age and went to college on a scholarship at the age of sixteen. After graduating with a B.S. in chemical engineering and an A.B. in African and Afro-American Studies, Mae attended Cornell Medical College, earning a doctorate in medicine in 1981. Hoping to apply her skills to help others, she traveled to West Africa as a Peace Corps medical officer. She then opened a medical practice in Los Angeles. In 1987

Mae joined NASA and trained to be an astronaut. Her journey on the space shuttle *Endeavor* in 1992 was groundbreaking for her as an African-American woman. Mae left NASA after six years to create the Jemison Group for Advancing Technology in Developing Countries. The company finds ways to improve people's lives using science and technology, enabling Dr. Jemison to use her knowledge for projects such as improving health care in Africa. Dr. Jemison wrote an autobiography, *Find Where the Wind Goes*, in 2001.

Jackie Joyner-Kersee Many consider Jackie Joyner-Kersee the best female athlete of all time. She was born in 1962 in East St. Louis, Illinois. After seeing a television movie about the great Babe Didrikson—who excelled at basketball, track and field, softball, and golf—Jackie decided to become a competitive athlete. Displaying her exceptional athletic gifts, she won the National Junior Pentathlon [five track and field events] Championship four times in a row. She received a basketball scholarship to UCLA, where she was an outstanding player. Her coach, Bob Kersee—later her husband—wanted to see her compete in multi-event contests. Jackie won a silver medal in the heptathlon [seven track and field events] at the 1984 Summer Olympics. In 1987 at the Goodwill Games in Moscow, she was the first woman ever to earn over 7,000 points. In 1988 she broke her own record at the Olympic Games in Seoul, winning the heptathlon gold medal and setting new records. Asthma and allergies did not prevent Jackie from achieving the goals that she had set for herself. She officially retired from competition in 2001.

Whitney Houston The daughter of a gospel singer (Cissy Houston) and cousin of a successful recording artist (Dionne Warwick), Whitney Houston was born in Newark, New Jersey, in 1963. Her vocal skills were apparent as she sang in the junior choir at her church. She developed her singing and dancing skills while maintaining a successful modeling career. Initially performing as a backup singer, Whitney launched a successful solo career with her self-titled 1985 album, the most successful debut solo album and album by a female African-American artist at that time. Her movie career flourished as well with her appearances in *The Bodyguard* (1992), *Waiting to Exhale* (1995), and *The Preacher's Wife* (1996). The recipient of many awards, including Grammys and American Music and NAACP Image awards, Whitney Houston supported numerous charitable causes. In 1989 she established the Whitney Houston Foundation for Children, Inc., a non-profit organization that benefits children around the world. In 1992 she married the singer Bobby Brown, and their daughter was born in 1993. Whitney Houston died in February 2012.